Have a New Family by Friday

A Practical Plan for a Happier Home in 5 Days

Dr. Kevin Leman

SAMPSON
RESOURCES

4887 Alpha, Suite 220 • Dallas, Texas 75244 • (972) 387-2806 • (800) 371-5248 • FAX (972) 387-0150
www.sampsonresources.com   info@sampsonresources.com

HOW TO USE THIS PARTICIPANT BOOK

This participant book is designed to accompany the *Have a New Family by Friday* video curriculum by Dr. Kevin Leman. Each lesson includes Scripture, Reflection (basic content of Dr. Leman's video presentations), Discussion, 5-Day Action Plan and Prayer. If you are participating in a group and are not able to complete all of the discussion in the time allotted, try to complete it at home or continue the next time the group is together. Discussion and interaction are key learning tools where participants benefit by sharing their own thoughts and insights. Keep in mind that the seven *5-Day Action Plans* have been thoughtfully designed to be practical and helpful. They are crucial to the study. If you will faithfully follow through with each of these plans, you will be on your way to a happier home. Best blessings as you seek to *Have a New Family by Friday!*

Scripture references: *The King James Version, The Living Bible, The New Living Translation*

Table of Contents

LESSON
1

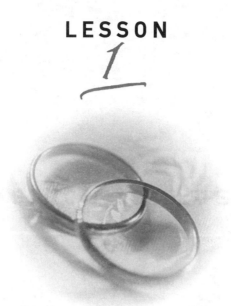

WHAT A DIFFERENCE A MARRIAGE MAKES!

Everything Works Better When the Marriage Is Working

SCRIPTURE:
Matthew 6:33
1 Peter 3:7
Ephesians 5:21-22, 25
Jude 21

REFLECTION

After being married for 46 years—in a row—to the same lucky woman—having five kids, grandkids, a busy speaking and writing schedule, I've learned a few things about family life! One thing I've learned about marriage is this: The kind of person you are at the core of your being, your spiritual values, and how you feel about life in general has everything to do with the kind of marriage and family you're going to have.

You may ask, "But can you really have a new marriage by Friday? We've been struggling for a long time." The answer is "Yes, you can! I promise: You really can!" In fact, you can have a new family by Wednesday! By sundown today—if you decide to do a few things differently and stick with it!"

I'm sure you're aware that our society is changing rapidly, but it's not all bad news. There's good news: The Word of God does not change! Now I'm not a Bible scholar—I'm a psychologist who tries to live by the Word of God. (Someone once said that if you took all the psychologists in the world and laid them end to end around the entire globe, it'd be a pretty good idea to leave them there!) But listen to the profound truth in Matthew 6:33. "Seek first the Kingdom of God and His righteousness, and all these things will be added to you." In other words, seek after goodness, joy and peace, and live an upright life, caring for one another with God's mighty Spirit working in you (Romans 14:17), and He will add to your life all you really need. I believe this applies to the marriage and family you need.

I think back often to when I was a young guy, standing at the altar shaking in my boots, my knees knocking, and this beautiful bride walks down the aisle toward me. And under her bouquet—I didn't realize it—was a "rule book"! And in that rule book was a lot of rules I was about to discover for the first time! I sometimes think that God was the original humorist when He said "And the two shall become one." Wow! How on earth were we going to pull that off?

Concerning marriage, here's a question for you: When the marriage ceremony takes place, how many people really get married? Two? Four? No, it's usually about six, because you marry a bunch of other people—your inlaws! You don't necessarily live with them, but they come with the package. And hopefully, this turns out to be a good thing. But sometimes it's challenging. If you happen to come out of a blended family, the number you "marry" changes from around six to ten or more. This can be even more challenging—but it can still work.

Now let's talk about four success factors that make marriage work better so that everybody in the home benefits. I could give you more than four, but let's focus on just four.

The first success factor is communication. The thing you have to understand about men and women is that they communicate differently. Women, for example, often conceal what it is they really want from us guys. For example, Sandy and I were driving home one night after dinner. We had declined dessert to save money. She turns to me and says, "Uh, you wanta stop for ice cream?" I answer "No" and keep driving. Ten seconds later, tears are running down her cheeks. "What's wrong?" I ask. "Nothing," she says. "What do you mean, 'nothing'? You're crying." "There's nothing wrong," she says again. "Well, something's wrong!" I say. She finally says, "I wanta stop for ice cream!" Women are interesting.

The point is: Women want you to know how they're feeling, gentlemen, without having to *tell* you how they're feeling. "Harold, will you come over and give me a hug?" Harold walks over and gives Sophia a hug. What does she say to herself? "Well, he hugged me all right, but only because I asked him to—not because he really wanted to."

Communication is the track that relationships run on—especially marriage relationships. You've got to share your thoughts, feelings, opinions, desires and beliefs freely with each other—without feeling that you're going to be put down, belittled, rejected or blown off. We'll talk more about communication later in the series.

A second success factor is transparency and authenticity. By this I mean openness and honesty with one another. When this is not present in marriage, trust between partners suffers and eventually disappears, and the ability to co-exist with confidence goes out the door. If you want that valuable close connection with your husband or wife, you've got to share the same core values—and at the top of the list are honesty, authenticity and a shared spiritual faith. Yes, women and men are very different—you've heard the differences—but they must share the same core values if they are to get along well, particularly the same *spiritual* values.

The person you are at your core will determine the kind of marriage and family you have.

A third success factor is an active, rewarding sex life. Look, I'm 69 years old. I mean I'm near death! At my age, I'm telling you, you slow down in some areas—physically, emotionally, sexually. But here's the kicker, to enjoy an rewarding sex life, certain conditions have to be met. The first thing Sandy and I did after we were married was to pull off the side of the road in a 1960 Corvair that burned 45 quarts of oil on the way to San Diego—and kneel at the side of the road and pray that God would bless our union—not bless our sex life. Forty-six years later—five kids—two grandkids—God answered our prayer. A rewarding sex life was a blessing.

A fourth success factor is spiritual oneness. When you consider marriage stats today, you find that the average marriage is cooked and done in seven years. Couples get married at about age 26 for women and 28 for men and are having babies later in life. Half of all marriages end in divorce. Sixty percent of those who get married between the ages of 20 and 25 end in divorce. If you were to examine these marriages closely, you'd see that they are lacking—particularly in shared spiritual values. Spiritual oneness means that you are in agreement on Christian values—your Christian faith, your church affiliation, your goals in life, your personal behavior and the example you set for your children.

Now let's talk about some **critical needs our wives have**. First Peter 3:7 tells us to "live with understanding" for a reason. *Among other things, wives especially need affection, understanding, support and communication.* Do husbands have to work at delivering on these? Yes. They're not natural for husbands at times. Wives need affection—not necessarily with sex—affection they hear, sense, see and feel. They need us to understand their opinions and frame of reference, and appreciate their common sense and wisdom. And they need to know that we have their backs, that they have our support emotionally, physically, spiritually and financially. They need us to communicate with them in more than grunts and sentence fragments, encouraging them, telling them we love and appreciate them and that we're just proud to be seen with them. They need to hear from us and see our words backed up with action. This is a quick summary, but guys, we've got to meet these needs our wives have.

What about the husband's needs? Wives, he needs your respect and admiration—your affection and romance that is so fulfilling to him—your companionship—and a peaceful atmosphere at home. He wants to be close to you and feel that you genuinely care about him and what he's dealing with. He doesn't want to be interrogated with question after question. It'll make him tend to clam up. Certainly questions are necessary, but instead of asking tons of questions, speak more in comments and observations, with something like "Oh, sounds interesting. Tell me more about it" or "I bet you've had a tough day. I can't believe all you have to do." He'll respond.

Believe it or not, most men don't have an abundance of friends. Know who they really want to be friends with? You. More than anything, they want to be close to *you*. They want you to be their best friend. (This may be the best thing I've told you.)

Ephesians 5:22 says, *"You wives must submit to your husband as you do to the Lord."* Then verse 25 says, *"And you husbands must love your wives with the same love Christ showed the church. He gave up his life for her."* But the best scripture of this little passage to me is verse 21 that says, *"Submit to one another out of reverence for Christ."* In other words, be respectful of each other, care for one another, and in so doing, you will be honoring Christ.

Wives, here's what I'd like you to understand. That husband of yours may burp—sit in boxer shorts in his recliner—watch two ballgames simultaneously—with a slice of pizza in one hand and a remote in the other—but he would take a bullet for you.

Now I understand that everybody participating in this study isn't married. Some have never been married, some are divorced or may be single parents; maybe some plan to be married. Whatever the case, understand this: The person you are at your core will determine the kind of marriage and family you have. Be an encourager, a listener, strive to meet each other's needs daily, pray together, stay honest and faithful, and *"always stay in the boundaries where God's love can reach and bless you"* (Jude 21).

Can you have a happier home in five days? Yes, you can. Follow the "5-Day Action Plan," and you'll be on your way to a happier home. I guarantee it! Everything works better when the marriage is working.

DISCUSSION

1. Reflect on the series title for a few moments and discuss as a group whether or not you think it's really possible to make significant changes for the better in a family—in just FIVE days. What kind of things have to happen? Make some notes.

   _____

   _____

   _____

2. Where does the burden of responsibility for positive change lie? With the kids? The neighbors? In-laws? Friends? Church? Employer? You'd have to agree that it's the responsibility of the _____ in the home to maintain control and set the pace. For married couples, you could say "as the _____ goes, so goes the home." Why is this so? Discuss together.

   _____

   _____

3. Recall and list below the "four key success factors" of marriage we mentioned in the video session. Maybe you want to add a couple of factors. Share some personal experiences that illustrate how important these factors are. Trust me—you don't want to miss on them!

a. _____

b. _____

c. _____

d. _____

4. I shared what I believe a *wife's* most important needs are. Now what do *you* think they are? Write your thoughts below and share with the group.

_____

_____

Are these needs being met? Are some not being met? As you feel comfortable, share those areas where you'd like to see improvement—areas that would benefit your marriage

5. Now let's consider the *husband's* important needs. Again, you've got my thoughts. What do *you* think his most important needs are? Are they being met?

_____

_____

5-DAY ACTION PLAN

DAY 1: Read Matthew 6:33 and discuss briefly as a couple what "seeking the Kingdom of God" and His "righteousness" means to you. Romans 14:17-19 tells us that the "Kingdom of God" is not a place or collection of people—it is a way of *"living a life of goodness and peace and joy in the Holy Spirit."* So today, **focus on each other's good qualities**—building each other up and purposefully maintaining a pleasant and peaceful home environment—through words and actions. If you are a believer in Jesus Christ, the Holy Spirit will enable you to create an environment where goodness, peace and joy reside, and everybody's comfortable. **Focus on each other's good qualities today.**

DAY 2: Meeting each other's needs is one of the most important success factors in a good marriage. **Today, identify what you think are your spouse's four or five deepest needs and focus on meeting at least ONE of them in a consistent way throughout the day.** If your focus today is "communication" or "conversation," make every effort to show an interest in what your spouse is interested in, i.e., the kids, household needs, job, health, etc. As you communicate, avoid excessive questioning and interrogating. Try to speak more

in statements, comments or observations. This often produces better responses than questions do. When it comes to "communication" and "conversation," remember that *how* you say what you say may be more important than *what* you say. Your tone of voice reflects your attitude—what you're really feeling inside. Don't blow a perfectly good day with a lousy attitude and tone of voice. **Today, identify what you think are your**

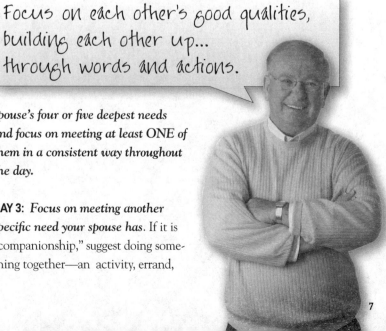

Focus on each other's good qualities, building each other up... through words and actions.

spouse's four or five deepest needs and focus on meeting at least ONE of them in a consistent way throughout the day.

DAY 3: *Focus on meeting another specific need your spouse has.* If it is "companionship," suggest doing something together—an activity, errand, dinner date, a trip to the mall, etc. Whatever you do, never let your spouse think you don't want to be with him. If the activity or errand really doesn't interest you, no problem. Do it anyway! The next time *you* seek companionship, your spouse will likely be agreeable. Just realize that hesitation or refusal over time can be interpreted as rejection, and companionship will begin to suffer. Point blank, say, "I want you to *be* with me. I need your help, your input, your thoughts…. " Afterwards, express gratitude by saying "Your being with me meant a lot, and I appreciate it." Today, *focus on meeting another specific need your spouse has*.

DAY 4: *Today, focus on still another specific need your spouse has*. If you're not sure what that need is, guess! You'll probably be right. If it's "affection" *and/or "intimacy,"* be attentive, thoughtful and helpful throughout the day. Avoid negative and critical attitudes and words—not just today—but every day. Stay positive and complimentary, sincerely expressing your feelings of attraction and affection toward your spouse. Romance and intimacy begin with positive attitudes

and kind words which lead to feelings of warmth and comfort between a husband and wife. *Focus on another specific need your spouse has.* Take action and see good results.

DAY 5: *Your action today is to show your respect and admiration for your spouse through words and deeds*. This matter of respect and admiration is often thought to be the husband's greatest need, but it is equally important to the wife. And it must be demonstrated. Today, make sure your spouse knows that you recognize her contribution to the home and family, and to your own life and sense of well-being. She does something for you that no one else can. You recognize her abilities and support, her intuition and care for you and the kids, along with her financial contribution if she works outside the home. Let her know that the family would be in a heap of trouble without her! Make sure she knows how much you appreciate and admire her. *Your action today is to show your respect and admiration for your spouse through words and deeds*.

PRAYER

Father, thank You for the assurance that You will help us make our marriage work as we commit our home and family to You. I promise to do my part to serve my family, communicating love and respect to each of them. Thank You for the blessing they are to me. In Jesus' name—Amen.

LESSON

2

WHAT A DIFFERENCE A MOM MAKES!

How a Mother's Influence Leaves an Indelible Imprint

SCRIPTURE:

Proverbs 31:10-31

Ephesians 6:1-3

REFLECTION

If there's a large group of young kids at a big event and suddenly there's an emergency that requires them to call for someone to come get them, who do you think they're going to call? Most of the time, their mom. Why? Because in most cases, she's the centerpiece and heartbeat of the family. When you've got a problem, call mom! "She'll feel my pain!"

In our first session, we talked about how society is changing. Well, the family is changing, too! Yet in spite of these changes, there's something about a mother that makes her want to rise to every occasion regardless of the changes going on around her. She's smart and intuitive; she's a communicator, an energized woman who has something built into her that makes her want to keep going and going. Down deep, she wants an intact family life where love and respect rule the day. And in her heart, she wants to have an influence that leaves an indelible imprint on her kids forever. Whether she's a married or a single mom, she

has the good of those children at heart. Here are some special thoughts for moms.

First of all, a mom is on duty 24/7! I remember when our kids were little, they were sick a lot, and my wife would sit patiently rocking those babies, taking care of them while I graded papers or worked on a manuscript. Many nights I got to do the rocking. I believe sharing those moments together is one reason we've had such a good marriage all these years.

Some time ago I was studying relationships and did a survey about the kinds of stress and degrees of stress women experience on a daily basis. My survey showed that the #1 stress in a woman's life was not the husband, the marriage or finances. It was the *children*. Was #2 the husband? No. It was *time*—specifically, the *lack* of it. *Husbands* came in at #3. (At least I wasn't #1.)

So my question to women is this: What about household duties, job, career, health, fitness, finances? Many women in the workplace today not only bring home the bacon—they fry it and wash the pan! So why are

9

household duties, money, finances, job, etc., farther down on the list? Because women are relational. They major in relationships—people—not things, especially while the kids are growing up. Women are "natural-born child-raisers"!

What does a "good" mom look like anyway? Proverbs 31 gives about as thorough a picture as you'd ever hope to see. Often referred to as the "Proverbs 31 woman," she's what you'd call the ideal woman, wife and mother. But is her description realistic in this crazy culture we live in? I think so.

Listen to this. A Proverbs 31 woman is virtuous and capable. She's trustworthy and enriches the lives of others, starting with her husband. She's a productive worker. She's energetic and strong. She's a great seamstress. (Well, these days when you've got Target and Walmart, maybe you can buy it cheaper than you can make it.) She's an entrepreneur. She possesses inner strength and dignity. She has a sense of humor and doesn't fear the future. In fact, imprinted on the back of her T-shirt are

Many women in the workplace today not only bring home the bacon—they fry it and wash the pan!

the words "No Fear." Mama Bear fears nothing. She says, "Mess with my cubs and you're toast!" She speaks with wisdom and kindness. She monitors everything going on in the home and within a wide radius of it!

What's the payoff for being a Proverbs 31 woman? Her kids will stand up and bless her. They're not just going give her a fist bump and a "Wh-sup, Mom?" They're going to rise up one day and applaud her—praise her—because they finally realize who buttered their bread all those years. They'll see her for the treasure she is. And the husband? If he's got a brain, he knows what he's got in her. His attitude is "If she ever decides to leave me, I'm going with her!"

Another thing about mom: She's a multi-tasker. She can juggle lots of things at the same time. That's what moms do. What about dad? Well, take me, for instance. I travel a lot, and when I'm on a business trip in a rental car, looking for an address, I have to turn off the radio, pull over and stop just so I can concentrate on the address. Sometimes dads can't multi-task

as easily as moms can.

Cooking was another challenge for me. I used to cook supper for the kids when my wife and oldest daughter had a store together. Instead of getting dinner to come out all at the same time, I'd yell, "Kids, come to dinner! The corn is ready!" Then 10 minutes later I'd yell, "The potatoes are ready." We ate in stages—I preferred calling them courses. That third course of fish sticks looked lonely on the plate.

Do men and women do life differently? Of course they do; but this is all part of God's plan—to take these two people who are drawn to each other, with different personalities and abilities, bring them together, and challenge them to live out their Christian faith and build a stable home.

Mom, I encourage you to pray for your kids daily. As a young guy who wanted no part of Christianity, I remember coming down every morning and seeing my mother in her favorite chair with her Bible open. She was either reading her Bible or praying—probably for me. I sure needed it. One way she blessed me was by praying for me and making sure I knew it. I honestly don't know how I'd have turned out had my mother not prayed for me. So mom, pray for your kids daily and make sure they know it.

Now here's a cornerstone scripture that applies to raising kids—Ephesians 6:1-3. It's a favorite of mine. The Apostle Paul must have been an "equal opportunity employer," because he talks to children first, then turns around and talks to parents. First, he says, *"Children, obey your parents,"* then he says (I'm summarizing), "And now a word to you parents: Don't keep scolding and nagging your kids, making them angry and resentful. Rather, bring them up with the loving discipline the Lord Himself approves of, with careful direction and godly advice." Again, I'm saying this in my own words.

Well, what if dad is missing from the home? What if you're a single mom? First of all, don't let guilt be your guide. Guilt can become the propellant for some bad decisions. Single mom, trust me—you can do this. Just be consistent and loving with your kids. Be watchful and attentive. There are *two* eyes watching over them instead of four. But hopefully, you've got some assistance from loyal relatives and friends. Set the boundaries, enforce them, be patient as your kids go through normal struggles, and apply the same good principles you would apply if the father were present in the home.

Plenty of godly women have raised terrific kids without a dad in the home. You can, too! Don't let yourself slip into a pity party. It won't help. Harness your inner strength and just do it. This applies to single dads, too.

A few other words of advice for single moms: Don't try to be both mom and dad. Mom, you don't have to run down and buy a hockey stick and a ball glove. Yes, there are things that surrogates such as uncles, grandfather, or a close Christian male friend can do to fill the gap, but they don't replace you as a mom. You're the voice. Be yourself, and be positive and hopeful. It will bolster the kids' self-esteem.

One more important point for single moms: Don't bad-mouth your ex. He may not be the right kind of guy, but don't rip on him. If you do, your kids might pay for it in the long run. If you have to move in with your family due to financial strain, don't give up your "mom-ship." Even if you're living with your parents, you're still the mom, and what you say goes. If you happen to be a grandparent in a situation like this, allow that daughter/mom to carry out her proper role. Give your support wholeheartedly. When our loved ones need help, we come through for them.

Now moms, have high expectations for your kids and make sure everybody in the family contributes to the well-being of the family. In today's culture, we have a tendency to turn our homes into hotels with room service, free laundry, snacks and a concierge floor for extra good behavior—with little expected in return. My be-lief is that children should have some responsibilities in the home. When they carry them out, you have a good reason to affirm them. And affirmation for achievement builds self-esteem.

One final thought, mom. Don't shy away from talking to your kids about sex—especially your son. Often that's left to the father. You want to teach kids the reality of what marital love is all about? Then here's a once-in-a-lifetime opportunity to do it—based on the teaching of God's Word. Don't wait too long to begin the process. My opinion is that age 9 to 12 is not too soon.

If you're having trouble with your kids—maybe they're teenagers—don't give up on them. I thank God often that my own mom persevered and didn't give up on me. She loved me in spite of the trouble I caused her. It reminds me the scripture that says, "nothing can separate us from the love of Christ." A mom's love runs deep.

If you're a mom who's wondering "When are these kids gonna straighten up and do right?"—you may not have an immediate answer. Just remember this: Set a godly example, pray for your kids, apply what we've talked about, and you've got solid shot at raising great kids.

Wow! What a difference a mom makes! Her influence leaves an indelible imprint that time simply cannot erase. We're grateful for our moms. And I'm grateful for you.

DISCUSSION

1. Discuss for a few moments the influence of the *mother* in the home you grew up in. What role did she play? What were some of her strengths that you admire?

_____

_____

_____

2. The "Proverbs 31 woman" is certainly to be admired. Reflect on some of her characteristics that you particularly identify with, and why. Which of these would you like to be characteristic of you? In which areas might you need to grow?

_____

_____

_____

3. What characteristics did you observe or lessons did you learn under your mother's influence that you have implemented or NOT implemented in your own home? Why or why not? Both women and men should join in the discussion as they feel comfortable.

_____

_____

4. What do you think are some of the most challenging issues facing moms in today's culture? Are things any different from when you were growing up? If so, how? Talk about needs and demands that require careful attention. Do you have any help?

_____

_____

5. Single moms have a huge responsibility, but can still raise outstanding kids. Share your own observations as to the challenges and possibilities they deal with. If you're a single mom, enlighten everybody! Your personal experiences will be encouraging.

_____

_____

6. Let's say you're an "experienced" mom whose kids have "turned out right," and you're asked to share five nuggets of advice to a group of young mothers. What would you say to them? You may think of more than five—but list at least five below. Share what you've written down.

a. _____

b. _____

c. _____

d. _____

e. _____

7. Finish this sentence: *In order to be the best influence I can possibly be on my kids and leave an indelible imprint on their lives, I need to…*

_____

_____

5-DAY ACTION PLAN

> Concentrate on that positive and godly image of the woman God wants you want to be.

DAY 1: In the process of carrying out your normal responsibilities with home and work, *focus on yourself today*—your blessings, your abilities, your possibilities and your potential. At the same time, consider the challenges you face. While those challenges may at times seem insurmountable, the inner strength you have through a relationship with Christ and the truths of the Bible will enable you to develop the same characteristics as the "Proverbs 31 woman." Your action today is to *focus on yourself*—think—envision—concentrate on that positive and godly image of the woman God wants you want to be.

DAY 2: *Focus today on the needs of your children* and try to understand how they *feel* about what they're dealing with. It's easy to lose touch. Depending on their age, they may need more more time and attention from you, activity with other kids, help with homework, a little extra spending money, a new CD, some advice, whatever? What are they thinking about, and how are you responding? Do they have to beg for help from you, afraid they'll be scolded or automatically see a "no" face and hear a "no" voice? Or do they feel totally comfortable coming to you with their needs, knowing that you of all people will be fair and thoughtful and ready to help them? Today, *focus on the needs of your children* and take positive action to meet them.

DAY 3: Give a gift to your kids today by *showing them through words and actions just how much you love and admire your husband—their father*. Create opportunities for the kids to see you and your spouse speak lovingly to each other, hold hands, kiss hello or goodbye. Sound mushy? Trust me, the biggest fear kids have is that their parents might split up! When they see you hugging or kissing, they may be saying "Yuk!" on the outside, but they're saying "Yippee!" on the inside. They're thinking, "They love each other and would never split up!" If you're single, let the children hear you speak affectionately to some special people in your life, i.e., the grandparents, relatives, close friends. Kids need to hear and see evidence of real love and commitment. *Mom, your action today is to show your kids through words and actions how much you love and admire your husband—their father*. If you're not married—show how much you love and respect the special people in your life.

DAY 4: Today, your action is to *communicate with your kids*—carrying on as much conversation with them as you possibly can. People we love and are comfortable

around, we spend time talking to. Engage the kids in conversation on topics they're interested in. Avoid excessive questioning, sermonizing, instructing, directing, bossing, intimidating, correcting, etc. This makes kids uncomfortable and tends to put them off. Instead of using questions, talk in statements, comment on events, share feelings, volunteer to help them, take them somewhere, and—very important!—keep a calm, non-threatening tone of voice. Don't always make your kids have to *ask* you for stuff. Offer ahead of time before they even have a chance to ask! Whatever you do, keep them talking to you. If they ever stop, you've got a problem. Today, *your action is to communicate with your kids*. Engage them in conversation.

DAY 5: *Today, zero in on your kids' attitudes, their friends, relationships, boundaries, school work, what's going on in their heads and world.* Know who they're hanging out with, where they're going and what they're planning to do when they get there, who's influencing them, etc. You say, "There's no way I can do all that!" Find a way! And do it without meddling and threatening. Just keep your eyes open, listen around, talk to other parents and use common sense. Don't slam your kids and their plans. If what they're planning isn't good, tell them so. Calmly say "I don't think this is best—it doesn't feel right. Let's think of some better options." Then get creative. Just don't *slam* them and *insult* them! Parents sometimes think they have the right to offend their kids. All it does is drive them smack into the arms of their peers whose parents are slamming them. Be firm, but with a gentle touch. *Today, zero in on your kids' attitudes, their friends, relationships, boundaries, school work, what's really going on in their heads and world.*

PRAYER

Father, I have the humbling responsibility and awesome privilege of being the godly mother my kids need. I promise to do my best to come through for them in the little ways as well as the big ways. I plan to leave an indelible imprint for good and for God on their lives. In Jesus' name—Amen..

WHAT A DIFFERENCE A DAD MAKES!

How a Father's Influence Leaves an Indelible Imprint

SCRIPTURE:

Ephesians 6:4

REFLECTION

I remember as a young man, sitting with Sandy in a restaurant where you could get a good steak for $3.99, and she gives me this little box. I'm thinking, "Well, hey! What is this?" I opened it up and inside were two little satin baby shoes. I looked at it and said, "Are we going to have a bubba?" Wow! I couldn't wait to be a dad. And after all these years, I can honestly say I've loved every minute of it.

Now I realize in talking to dads, I'm not talking to just married dads. You may be a single dad, a grandfather, or not even a dad yet. Researchers tell us that a father's influence is so strong that some women who didn't have an adequate father figure develop what is called "father hunger." Without a good father figure, they *invent* one. Ultimately, we all want good relationships in life, and dads who are engaged in their children's lives prepare them for developing those relationships. When there's an engaged dad in the home, kids develop higher self-esteem, fewer behavioral problems, less chance of get-

ting into drugs, and a healthier concept of God. It's a proven fact.

There's a profound word for dads in Ephesians 6:4. The Apostle Paul tells fathers not to provoke or antagonize their kids and make them angry. Instead, bring them up in the training and instruction of the Lord—teaching them the ways of God. When your kids look up at you, what do they see? They should see something of what God is like. Why? Because you're trying to live as Christ would have you live.

If you have a daughter, and she's curious as to what God is like, she should be able to look at you and get a good idea. If you have a son who wonders what God is like, he should be able to look at you and get his answer. You ought to make your goal in life to represent God in your home through how you speak and carry yourself. That's really what being a Christian father is all about.

Not all dads represent God well in the home. Some are critical, in-your-face, know-it-all guys who rule with an iron fist. That's how they were raised, so they're going to raise their kid the same way. Well, the truth is, if you want to plant the seeds of rebellion in your kid's life, dad, that's how you do it. By knowing it all, being loud, highly opinionated, always right, rigid and unthoughtful. Just remember, with extreme rigidity comes extreme resistance. Plant a crop of rigidity and you'll grow a crop of resistance—the very thing you don't want from your kids.

Dad, when it comes to building a good relationship with your kids, let me tell you something. You can win big with your wife, your kids, your colleagues at work, and in your relationships if you'll just make a habit of speaking kindly and respectfully to them. (That may be the best thing I tell you in this entire series. I mean that.) A manly, courageous—but—kind and thoughtful father is pure gold in the home!

Think about it. What if dads spoke to their best customers the way they speak to their wives and kids? Hopefully, it would be fine. But in many cases, those customers and clients would scram like mice in a roomful of cats. God gave us free will to say and do whatever we want within the law. But just because you and I sit behind the steering wheel of life doesn't mean it's OK to say and do whatever we please. There's a price to pay for that, and everybody pays. Let's be careful what we say and how we say it.

Here's a good word for dads and moms by educator Elizabeth Harrison. She said, "The people who are lifting the world onward and upward are those who encourage more than they criticize." **Instead of criticizing in detail and praising in general, try praising in detail and criticizing in general.** In other words, stay focused on the positive, and there won't be enough time to focus on the negative. Reinforce good behavior more and more, and unacceptable behavior less and less; and soon the unacceptable behavior will tend to fall by the wayside.

Think about this: Professional animal and bird trainers have practiced this concept of reinforcing good behavior and NOT focusing on incorrect behavior for hundreds of years. Do you think a trainer teaches a whale to roll on its side and splash water on a crowd of kids at Sea World by hollering at him or punishing him when he doesn't do it right during training exercises? Do you think a trainer teaches three dolphins to shoot up out of a pool, do perfectly-timed coordinated flips high in the air by positive reinforcement when they do it right

or by punishing them when they do it wrong? You know the answer. These mammals quickly learn that good things (treats) happen when they do things right. So why would they ever *want* to do things wrong? Positive reinforcement works!

Dad, another thing: **You need to be a good listener.** In general, we men don't listen too well. I can't tell you how many times I've shown up at the wrong restaurant, and I'm saying, "My wife is late again!" I call her and she says, "Lemmie, Lemmie, Lemmie, where are you?" I answer, "I'm over at *Outback*." "Well, buddy boy, we had this conversation, and I told you to be …." OK, I'm not a great listener.

When our kids lose their way, we go find them, bring them home and care for them.

Now have I learned to become a *better* listener as the years go by? Yes, I have. And, hopefully, you have, too. Listen to your kids and "hear" what they're really saying. Too often they see this giant mouth spouting out words they don't understand on subjects they don't relate to—when what they need to see are two giant ears that catch every word they say. Dad, your role is uniquely different from mom's, but in a good way. Your role should be complementary to hers. Again, it's a matter of making our differences work for us for the benefit of our children and the well-being of the family.

Dad, let me ask you a personal question: Do you see yourself as a leader? Regardless of your answer, **you need to be a leader**—and you need to know *who* you're leading. Consider the Good Shepherd who went way out of His way for the one sheep who'd gone astray. That's how we're to be as dads. We lead with a firm but gentle spirit, hand and heart because we care. When our kids lose their way, we go find them, bring them home and care for them. I think wives look at their husbands every day and ask this question: "Do you really love me? Do you really care about me and these kids?" They'll get their answers through the way you care, listen and communicate with them.

A couple of quick questions here: 1) **Do your kids see joy in your life, dad?** They ought to. It will heighten their self-esteem. Are you super critical, always pointing out your kid's flaws? If you do, they may never feel like they measure up. 2) **Do you bless your children?** Do they hear you speak your approval of them, recognizing when they're doing something right? Tell them you're proud of the way they're coming along, how thoughtful they are to want to reach out to a kid who can't afford tickets to the school event. "Honey, you're going in the right direction. What you're doing is so important. Can I help you with it?" Call your wife on the way home from work and say, "Babe, do you need me to stop by the store and pick up something for you?" Coming from a husband and dad? Man, little stuff like that is gold! You're "blessing" them and showing your approval when you do this kind of thing.

I'll say this more than once in this study because it's so important, but here it is, dad. **Learn to *respond* instead of *react*.** There's a big difference between the two. If your daughter comes home with a streak of blue hair, don't blow your top. If your son comes to you with a proposal that seems a little crazy, don't make him feel stupid. He'll think twice before he comes to you again. Instead of reacting, respond. Say something like, "Hey, tell me more about what you're thinking… or let's think it through together…or…if it's not possible, maybe we can work something out that's better." If you go to the doctor, and he says you've *reacted* to the medication, is that good or bad? It's bad. If he says you've *responded* to the medication, is that good or bad? It's good. This principle is the same with kids, wives and everybody. Be a *responder*—not a *reactor*, and others will enjoy being around you more.

What's your mouth like, dad? Do you use bad language at home and derogatory terms about other people? If you do, shame on you. It's harmful, and everybody loses. Especially your kids. They're watching you and listening to you. Single dad, don't bad-mouth your ex. I don't care what she's like or how much you've been hurt. Don't do it. Dad, do you demonstrate an exaggerated self-importance before your wife and kids? Don't do it. Instead, project a sincere attitude that you've still got things to learn and that you make mistakes, too. And finally, a real dad can say "I'm sorry—forgive me" when he's wrong.

One day after I spoke to a big Pepsi Cola function, a guy came up to me afterwards and said, "Hey, Kevin, something I've learned is that everybody has to win and *feel* like a winner in my organization." Your kids want to feel like winners. Let them know that you're out to help them win in life.

In closing, let me just say this: **You don't ever stop being a dad.** It's an ongoing process. But that's good. We can make an indelible imprint on our kids and home—if—IF—we stay faithful to Christ in our daily attitude and walk. Send your daughter flowers for a special achievement—and what will she think? Knock yourself out for that son who's down in the dumps because he struck out every time at bat in the game—and what will he think? Tell your kids you're surprising your wife with a special night out—and what will they think? I tell you what they'll think: "That's one fine dude right there!" What will mom think, "That man is a sweetheart! He's gonna be glad he took me out!"

This isn't rocket science, friend. Being a good dad makes a big difference. A happier home awaits you.

DISCUSSION

1. If you grew up in a home where the dad was present, what were some of his characteristics that made an impression on you? How was authority balanced in the home? Talk about it.

_____

_____

_____

2. As a dad, what are some of your biggest hopes and dreams for your children? Are you seeing any evidence of progress toward them? Jot them down and be specific.

_____

_____

_____

What are some areas of concern—perhaps even fear—for your kids as they move out into the future and why? Again, try to be specific.

_____

_____

3. It seems that today, all kinds of influences are competing for our children's attention and loyalty—much of it negative and harmful. What are some of the influences you're watching out for as a dad? What are you doing about them? What *can* you do without turning your kids off?

_____

_____

4. Discuss with the group some specific things you can do as a dad to show your wife and kids how much you appreciate them. Be creative, but realistic.

_____

_____

5. If your son or daughter were asked to write a line or two saying what they loved and admired most about you—their dad—*what would you want them to say?* Think carefully and jot down a thought or two..

_____

_____

6. You'd agree that there are many things dads do that influence their kids' lives. In the space below, write what you consider to be "five crucial things" you *must* do as a dad to leave a positive and lasting imprint on your children's lives.

a. _____

b. _____

c. _____

d. _____

e. _____

5-DAY ACTION PLAN

DAY 1: Today—just like we asked the moms to do—*focus on yourself and the kind of person are you.* If you're married, are you a faithful and thoughtful husband? Whether you're married or not, are you a man of high moral character and integrity? Are you heavy-handed and controlling, always right? Are you fully engaged in your children's activities? Do you try to set the tone and pace of the home by leading an exemplary Christian life before your wife and kids? Is your temperament such that kids can come to you and be treated with openness and respect? Today, *focus on yourself and the kind of person you are.* After making changes that are needed, everyone in your home will see the difference.

> Today you need to monitor your attitude and tone of voice around the house.

DAY 2: *Today, project a warm, open and loving attitude around your home and family.* Do you give your kids adequate attention, engage them in conversation and activity at their level of understanding, have realistic expectations, have a "yes" face that says "I'm open to whatever's on your mind"—or do you ignore them and pretty much let them do their own thing while you do yours? After all, you're a busy man, under more pressure than they'll ever know. Do you listen to your kids and value their thoughts, ideas, proposals and opinions so they feel appreciated and important? Do you *react* negatively or *respond* positively to their inquiries and proposals? Today, do your best to **project a warm, open and loving attitude around your home and family** through a calm and friendly tone of voice.

DAY 3: Today, *make it obvious to your children how much you love and appreciate their mother.* Kids thrive on this. Nothing means more to them than seeing evidence of love and affection between their mother and father. On the other hand, nothing hurts them more than seeing conflict, hearing harsh, unkind words and hurtful exchanges between mom and dad. They don't forget it easily, and tend to live on the edge, wondering when and where it will happen next. Don't—DO NOT—let this happen in their presence! Ever! Instead, look for ways to show thoughtfulness and appreciation for your wife—how much you love her by words and acts of affection like hugs and kisses the kids can see. It makes them feel secure, and you'll be their hero! *Today,* **make it obvious to your children how much you love and appreciate their mother.**

DAY 4: Today, *focus on how you relate to your children in terms of their behavior.* Do you see your kids' behavior simply as being *good* or *bad*? If it's good, you say, "Well, that's good." If it's bad, you automatically say, "Well, punishment's on the way!" Hold on a minute. What about stopping to realize that children are children and that there are alternatives to punishment? Kids do what they do because they think the way they think. They don't think like adults. They can't. When a 7-year-old "misbehaves," often what he's really doing is just being a 7-year-old. Little kids leave their toys scattered around the room because they're little kids. That's what little kids do. *With time, patient teaching, and more focus on discipline than punishment, they will learn to do better.* What about teenagers? Don't expect them to think like you do. They don't know what you know and haven't been where you've been. They're struggling just learning how to be a teenager. The key is to observe your kids' behavior—normal, acceptable, good, unacceptable, improving, whatever—and patiently guide them to a level of behavior that's appropriate for where they are in life. Make sense? Today, **focus on how you relate to your children in terms of their behavior.**

DAY 5: Your action today is to **set your mind on an image of what you want your kids to "be" when they're ready to leave home as adults.** It's one thing to want them to "turn out right"—it's quite another thing to have a clear vision of what you want them to be in terms of Christian character, moral values, self-esteem and personal convictions—and rear them with this vision clearly in mind. It's like the old line that says, "If you don't know where you're going, any old map will get you there." What do you want to see in your kids? How do you want them to turn out? Are you raising them to be "respectful, responsible and resourceful"? Are they going to leave home feeling good about their family and upbringing, grateful for the examples their mom and dad set before them, and confident they can "do life" well? Throughout this day, **set your mind on an image of what you want your kids to "be" when they're ready to leave home as adults.** From this point on, rear your kids with that image in mind. It will pay off big time!

PRAYER

Father, my biggest concern of the moment is that I follow through with this action plan—not just for five days, but forever. Write it on my heart and mind so I can be the best influence possible on my children. I know they deserve it. In Jesus' name—Amen.

LESSON
4

CHORE LIST

✓ Take out trash

✓ Clean Room

✓ Feed pet

WHAT A DIFFERENCE DISCIPLINE MAKES!

It's Now or Never—You Don't Have Forever

SCRIPTURE:

Proverbs 22:6

REFLECTION

There's a tall church steeple located in north Dallas, Texas, that's one of the most beautiful you'll ever see. And on all four sides of the steeple is a clock; and under the clock are the words "Night Cometh." What do you think the message of that short phrase is? Well, it means that life is temporal—it's limited—time is running out for all of us. When it comes to this matter of discipline, we're talking about teaching, training, developing, exercising self-control. Of course, the best discipline of all is self-discipline. The point is, we have a short window to instill discipline in our kids, because soon they'll be up and gone. We have to do it now while we still have time.

One thing we all agree on: We want our kids to be well-behaved. But go sit in a park or mall and watch kids. You'll see why some mothers are pulling their hair out! Their kids act like a bunch of monkeys on Mountain Dew! Kids shorter than a yardstick are in charge of adults! It's crazy! I'm old enough to remember when kids

used to obey their parents. Now parents obey their kids!

The scripture I've chosen for this lesson is a familiar one—Proverbs 22:6. *"Train up a child in the way he should go, and when he is old, he will not depart from it."* You can quote it by heart. I hope it will take hold in your life in a fresh, new way.

Are we training our kids UP today, or are we training them DOWN? I think too much of the time we train them DOWN. We think for them, make decisions for them, do their chores for them, speak on their behalf, do their homework, answer the questions other people are asking them, and on I could go. This, my friend, is not training a kid UP—it's training a kid DOWN. We yap, yap, yap at them instead of getting their attention to reason with them and explain things to them. Training UP is not a snap of the fingers. It's a carefully thought-out process of leading kids to think for themselves, reason things out, make their own decisions, clarify their own thoughts, express their needs, explain their actions, answer their own questions and achieve their own good results. Whew! Now to me, that's training a kid UP. And you know what? Training kids UP reflects parental confidence. Training kids DOWN reflects parental insecurity. Think about it.

Some people preach instant obedience, instant progress. Well, that's not how life works. Training UP takes time—especially when you're training a daughter or son in the way she or he should go. The lesson here is that kids come into the world wired differently. God has designed them to excel in different areas—areas that are *right* for *them*. Our job as parents is to help them find that area, develop that skill or talent so they can excel in it. And we need to get on with process. "Night cometh."

I'm old enough to remember when kids used to obey their parents. Now parents obey their kids!

My book *Making Children Mind Without Losing Yours* has sold over a million copies for a reason. It's a very practical book with Ephesians 6:1-4 as its foundation. Now it's a good book title, but we don't really *make* children mind, do we? We lead children to understand how to develop self-control and function in a way that is acceptable and proper for where they are in life. See, we parents tend to think there's *good* behavior and there's *bad* behavior. But there's also *normal* behavior—normal for where kids are in life. It's not normal for a 5-year-old to slam-dunk a basketball, so there's no need chewing him out when he can't do it. It's normal for your little daughter to do the same wrong thing time after time, because that's how her mind works where she is in life. Now, the challenge is to keep up with their development process and lead them to appropriate behavior based on where they are in life. You have to monitor their thinking, actions, progress, and guide them patiently. Their built-in desire is to one day be independent of you, so you need to lead them toward independence. If you don't do it now, you might not have a chance to later. Night cometh.

Talking about behavior and such—what if we spoke to and treated dinner guests in our home like we do our kids? Think about that. You've got two couples from church coming over for dinner. Your wife's made a beautiful pork tenderloin dinner, and everybody's ready to dig in. Suddenly you turn to your guest on the right and ask, "Did you wash your hands?" To another, "Did you put your napkin in your lap!" To another, "You're chewing with your mouth open. The neighbors next door can hear you eating!"

My point is: Your kids are people; they have feelings; and you either draw them into the family or you push them out the door. And, speaking of that, do you know the statistics on kids staying involved in church once they leave home? Well, they're dropping out like leaves in hailstorm! So, are we doing things well in the home? In some cases, great; but in many cases, not great.

Outside influences are putting unbelievable pressures on kids. Years ago, Homer Simpson replaced Ward Cleaver. (Do you know who Ward Cleaver is?) Watch how dads get bashed in sitcoms. Watch how the local minister is pictured as a doofus in movies! Secular media, the Internet, entertainment venues, smart phones, video games, and social media are opening up a world of experience that is coming at our kids like a Tomahawk missile. The lesson here: You're not the only one "raising" your kids today. You've got help! Better wise up to what's zooming in on those kids you're trying hard to raise right. Consider smart phones: The world's information and personalities are available to kids in words, pictures, sound and video. Unless kids are trained right, that can be a scary thought.

What I'm saying is, parents, hold your kids close. Monitor what they're learning, picking up here and there, and who's influencing them. Don't entrust them to every activity and everybody who's got a "wonderful program for your gifted child. Why it's only $200 a month for three nights a week." Again, YOU are going to make the primary difference in how your kids turn out, not someone outside the home.

Let's get back to this matter of behavior and the fact that the clock is ticking on how much time you have left to train your kids. And keep in mind, I'm not trying to run a military camp here. I just want you to know that kids need to be held accountable for the things they do in life in relation to "where they are" in life. This mother said to me, "Dr. Leman, my son is just willfully disobedient." That was her term. I ask, "Why do you say that? Did he do something that makes you say that?" "Well, he was pulling books off a shelf, and I told him 'No! No! Stop doing that!' He looked right at me, Dr. Leman, and just pulled another book off!" I said, "Well, what did you do then?" She said, "Well, I walked over there and smacked him a good one! Made him cry!" I said, "Well, let me ask you a question. How old is your son?" "He just turned one last week."

Let me tell you something about "developmentally appropriate behavior." It's fun. It's developmentally appropriate for a 1-year-old to throw food on the floor, or pull a $200 vase off a table and break it. He gets a kick out of it. It's like a firecracker going off. It excites him. Coloring on the dining room wall is fun! She loves it! Parents, listen, kids do stuff like that at a young age. Don't put a $200 vase within reach of the child. Don't give her crayons—give her finger paint. You'll see some real art!

Why does a kid throw a temper tantrum in the church vestibule on Sunday morning? He wants to get his way. You walk into Walgreens, and she wants a candy treat that you won't let her have. She throws a tantrum, wallowing on the floor. Why? She's saying, "I'm in authority over you, and you're gonna do what I want you to do, or you're gonna have to listen to this!"

Ephesians 6 teaches that God has placed YOU in authority over the children, not the children over you. And that's where you need to right the ship, today, in your parenting. You draw those lines in as many places as you can. In some places, you just step over the situation, without abandoning the child or need of the moment.

What do you do with a 16-year-old who says, "I'm not going to church anymore!" Do you just let him do his own thing? Or do you say, "Son, I accept the fact that you don't want to go to church—that you think the kids down there are not very friendly. But here's the thing—your dad and I have discussed this, and we really don't ask you to do a lot of things you don't enjoy. But, in about an hour and 20 minutes from now, when I look down the pew and see you sitting down the row from me, just know that your dad and I appreciate the fact that you respect us and have done the right thing. So shuffle off now and get ready. We're leaving shortly." That's how I'd handle it—calmly, but firmly—acknowledging his feelings, but with the positive expectation that he's going to do the right thing.

Kids misbehave for several reasons. One reason is that they want attention. It's normal. Your son or daughter will try to get attention in your home by doing positive

things or negative things. Whatever works. Sometimes kids misbehave because they're discouraged. They misbehave because they've seen a lot of misbehavior in the home. They've decided it works sometimes. You know, discipline applies to the parents as well as the kids. And we parents don't have forever to learn that either. Night cometh.

What about power-driven kids? Sometimes they feel like they've been so hurt in life, they have a right to strike out at other people. We've seen the results of this in the mass shootings. "I only count when I'm the boss—when I control things—when I win—when I dominate instead of everybody else dominating me— I'm sick of it!" In my book *Parenting the Powerful Child* that's coming out next year, I say to parents, "If you've got a powerful child at home, you've got a powerful parent somewhere." Kids don't learn to be powerful out of thin air.

> Keep your kids talking to you so they won't turn away and shut you out of their lives.

Is Proverbs 22:6 talking about being powerful? No. Does God grab us by the scruff of the neck and twist our earlobe and tell us we're going to do this or that? Not exactly. But believe me, He can get our attention. Yet through it all, He loves us. He's patient with us. He forgives us. And if we are professing believers in Christ, He looks upon us as if we've never even sinned. Now there's a powerful thought!

Want to see discipline flourish in your home? Listen to each other. Keep your ears open more than your mouth. Look for the good your kids do, their thoughtfulness, their developing character traits. Keep the home environment comfortable. Minimize questioning your kids. Don't use threatening language. And don't feel that you have to keep every threat you make, because sometimes you make the wrong threat. Keep a wrong threat, and you may be sorry. Model forgiveness. Offer praise and encouragement that's meaningful and not shallow. Keep conversation going on whatever is important to the kids. Keep your kids talking to you so they won't turn away and shut you out of their lives. Make them feel like you're the best and most loyal friend they'll ever have—that you'd fight hell with a water pistol for them! You're not looking for perfection. You just want them to grow up knowing it's best to do what's right.

What's the lesson here? Train kids UP, teach them UP, grow them UP—toward that positive image you have of them when they're ready to leave home. Remember: It's now or never—you don't have forever. If you want a happier family, discipline makes a big difference. Night cometh.

DISCUSSION

1. Discuss for a few moments why this lesson was not titled "What a Difference Punishment Makes!" instead of "What a Difference Discipline Makes!" Talk about it together?

   • Punishment suggests _____

   • Discipline suggests _____

   Which of the two do you think Proverbs 22:6 is referring to? _____

2. What about your own upbringing? Were you raised in an environment where punishment was certain if you didn't walk the line? Or were your raised where teaching and training were emphasized so you would learn to "stay" in line? Share some of your experiences.

   _____

   _____

   _____

3. What we're talking about in this lesson is getting kids to do what? Be perfect? Never mess up? Always do exactly the right thing? What are we trying to achieve here? Be specific.

   _____

   _____

   _____

4. In the Scriptures we see the term "disciple" used primarily as a noun. Discuss for a moment Jesus' relationship with His disciples. What was He trying to achieve with them? What does the word "disciple" mean to you as a verb? Share your thoughts.

   _____

   _____

   _____

5. Discuss what the subtitle to this lesson suggests to you. Realistically, how long do parents have before other influences begin to pull hard at kids? Is the "pull" at work now? What are you doing to get your kids to listen to you respectfully and live by the standards you've set?

   _____

   _____

   _____

6. What do you feel are the major types of teaching, training and instruction kids need today? If they don't get it at home, where are they going to get it?

_____

_____

_____

7. This matter of discipline applies to more than just kids. It applies to everyone in the home—adults included—married, single, never married. Mention a few important summary points in this lesson that resonated with you.

_____

_____

_____

5-DAY ACTION PLAN

DAY 1: Your action today is to *reflect on your own concept of discipline and how it came to be*. Ask yourself, "What difference does it really make anyway? What's the long-range payoff? Discipline is about kids—doesn't have much to do with me." Did you grow up in a home where everybody got along well? Were things done on a timely basis and in an orderly way? Did you grow up understanding the value of <u>self</u>-discipline? Think about what it means to "disciple" a new believer in Christ. You're familiar with that terminology and may have discipled others spiritually yourself. Consider the concept of "discipline" more along the line of "discipling"—training, teaching, developing—instead of just being organized and methodical. How has discipline made a difference in your life personally? *Today, reflect on your own concept of discipline and how it came to be.*

DAY 2: *Evaluate how you "discipline," then make changes as necessary.* Examine your own level of discipline as a man, woman or parent in the various areas of life. Are you expecting more of others than you are of yourself? Are you focusing on teaching, training and guiding your children, helping them develop self-control? Or do you tend to focus more on punishing when someone messes up? Do you try to "catch your kids doing something right" or "catch them doing something wrong"? Are you affirming your kids, recognizing their achievements, and encouraging them to move forward? Encouragement itself is a kind of discipline, multiplying the good that people are capable of. Family members flourish in an encouraging environment. Again, discipline applies to adults just like it does to kids. *So today, evaluate how you "discipline," then make changes as necessary*.

DAY 3: Discipline can be applied to several areas of life—some we haven't even talked about. Today, I'd like you to *focus on financial discipline, especially as it applies to your kids.* In challenging economic times, discipline pays off. Whether you're living on little, just enough, or plenty, your kids need to be developing values related to money and how to handle it. Are they contributing to the family in ways children can, with chores that make mom and dad's lives a little easier? Do they have part-time jobs? Do they understand what mom and dad go through to provide for them, and do they appreciate it? Big lessons can be learned in good times and hard times. *Focus on financial discipline today, especially as it applies to your kids*.

DAY 4: Hopefully, today will be a walk in the park for you—literally. I want you to *consider discipline as it*

> Whether you're living on little, just enough, or plenty, your kids need to be developing values related to money and how to handle it.

applies to the health and fitness of everyone in your family. After two knee replacements, walking two miles a day is a chore for me; but I have to do it. And I eat like a bird—well not like a canary—more like a large sparrow. But at age 69, exercise for me is a must. Are you disciplined in ways that benefit your health? Are you teaching your kids to be disciplined in terms of diet and exercise? Encourage them by example to take care of themselves. In our culture today, possibilities for success are often related to how people take care of themselves. This is hard to do with kids unless mom and dad are disciplined. If you talk the talk, you've got to _____ the _____! Walk together, exercise together, ride the riding lawnmower together! Today, *consider discipline as it applies to the health and fitness of everyone in your family*. I'm right there with you.

DAY 5: Today, *focus on striving for a more disciplined spiritual life*. Hopefully, this is an area where you are strong. If not, I challenge you to make God's Word the frame around the canvas on which your day is painted. And not just today, but every day from this day forward. Choose a Bible reading or devotional plan. Many are available online. Also, consider God's plan and purpose for your life. Do you sense His leading and direction? Are you sharing your life and experiences helping others grow? Are you living in such a way that others can tell you are a Christian woman, man or young person? I hope you're involved in a good church where the Bible is taught and people fellowship with each other. Today, *focus on striving for a more disciplined spiritual life*. Nothing you can do will bless your home more.

PRAYER

Father, there's room in my life for more discipline, certainly in the area of my personal relationship with You. I want to grow as a Christian and set a worthy example for my family. I'm trusting You to lead me in the paths I should go. In Jesus' name—Amen.

WHAT A DIFFERENCE ATTITUDE MAKES!

Helping Teenagers Navigate the Perfect Storm of Adolescence

SCRIPTURE:

James 1:26

Proverbs 15:1

Romans 12:2

REFLECTION

A few years ago I did a video series called *Running the Rapids* where we talked about how parents are like the whitewater guide who has to "know the river, know the raft, know the rocks, know the riders, know the rewards" and so on. The guide standing on the back of the raft is the only thing keeping the riders from winding up in the drink! So it is with parents whose task it is to help their kids make it safely through the rapids of adolescence. Now I've been in one of those rafts in Colorado. I did exactly what that guide said to do—"paddle hard left, both sides forward, paddle hard right, big boulder under water just ahead!" Was I ever glad to get out of that rubber tub! Know who got us safely down that river? I did! Just kidding. The guide did.

Now in this lesson, we're focusing again on teenagers—and parents—and the difference "attitude" makes in getting everybody through the teenage years. Do all teenagers have attitude problems? Certainly not.

Do parents? Thankfully not. Some families make it through these years like a cool breeze blowing down a fairway on a summer evening. But all too often, the adolescent years are more like a sand trap, high weeds or a muddy creek bed to lots of families. And it's downright devastating to many of them. In fact, if families aren't careful, adolescence can turn into a "perfect storm."

You've probably read the book or seen the movie *The Perfect Storm*. Just recently we saw the havoc a perfect storm unleashed on the east coast, New Jersey and New York. Meteorologists tell us three things have to come together simultaneously to create a one of these beasts: 1) a hurricane; 2) a high pressure system; and 3) a low pressure system. When these three weather systems collide, you've got a storm that's catastrophic!

What does this have to do with rearing teenagers? Consider these three components coming together: 1) teenagers themselves—their physical, emotional, social, intellectual, and spiritual development; 2) the pressure from peers who are saying, "Get with us, man; drink this, snort that, it won't hurt you, your parents will never know—they don't care anyway;" and 3) the pressure from parents who often over-control, don't know how to handle their kids, and are struggling with their own issues. When these three components come together, you've got the makings of a "perfect storm" in the home. My goal in this lesson is to help you avoid it.

So what does "attitude" have to do with all of this? Well, for a parent like you, a lot—because you're the "guide" in the back of the raft. How you relate to your kids and where they are in life is everything. First of all, you're an adult. You've been through a lot, know a lot, and have life experience on your side. So more is expected of you than is expected of the kids. Let's focus on you and what you can do to prepare for those critical developmental years. Believe me, they can be a barrel of fun. So how do you get there? As Tarzan once said to Jane: "Grab a vine." Here are some vines to grab hold of.

...if families aren't careful, adolescence can turn into a "perfect storm."

Make friends and *stay* friends with your kids. How do you do that? Treat them like you treat your closest adult friends or your best customers. You say, "But they're adults, and that's different." Well, just because your kids are "your" kids doesn't mean you can treat them disrespectfully. It's no wonder some kids can't wait to have their own room, TV and smart phone. They want to retreat to it and get away from their folks. It's true that parents hold the authority, have the gold and make the rules. But, hey, whatever happened to setting the tone of the home with a positive attitude, openness to everyone's thoughts and opinions—even their music, without slamming it? And again, the earlier you start this, the better off you'll be. Actually, you should start preparing before your kids are old enough to cry.

As soon as your kids begin coming to you proposing this or that, start *responding* early with things like:

- Tell me what you think. I'm all ears.
- If anybody can figure this out, you can.
- Makes sense to me. Tell me more.

- That's an interesting idea you've got there.
- I need your opinion. How does this tie look?
- Just let me know if you need any help with that.
- You know I'm always open to you.

If you want your kids to be close to you, make yourself pleasant to be close to. They're dealing with some uncertainty as they approach adolescence and desperately want to be included with the "right people." But guess what? You've got to be at the top of that "right people" list.

Want to turn your kids off? Start *reacting* early with things like this:

- That sounds like another one of your crazy ideas!
- Now that was a dumb thing to ask!
- The answer was NO and still is NO! Zip it!
- How many times do I have to tell you!
- There you go again! Just what I expected!
- You know the answer, so why even ask?!
- If a bird had your brain, he'd fly sideways!

Did you notice that the first list consists of *positive responses*, and the second consists of *negative reactions*? You know what's at the base of responses and reactions? A way of thinking, feeling and attitudes that reveal themselves in words and actions. Believe it or not, kids start picking up on it soon after they're born. They figure out who's who and what's what. Kids want a welcoming environment, a comfortable place to grow up in, and they want it to be with YOU—until it becomes uncomfortable.

Ever watch Animal Planet and see underwater footage of a baby whale swimming alongside its mother, tracking her every move? That baby knows where the goods are. Listen, parent, your kids want to be close to you. Please believe me and don't take this lightly: You provide everything in their existence—what they eat, wear, play with, sleep in, ride in, you name it. They have no assets but you. You are their source, and they know it. As long as you've got something to offer them, they'll swim alongside you—right through high winds and turbulent waters while other kids are fighting just to stay afloat.

Is this realistic? You bet it's realistic! "Do I give up my position of authority in the home?" No. You must be in *authority* over your kids—just don't be an *authoritarian* who's got to pull every string in their journey to independence. That's a sign of insecurity, not security.

Be their friend from day one and do your best to keep it that way. Turn them off, and they'll tune you out.

Talk about the heavy-handed authoritarian—I heard about a dad who didn't approve of his teenage daughter's record collection, so he gathered up all her CDs in her presence, took them into the back yard, put them in a fire box and burned them right in front of her! Said they were evil. True story. My question is: If they were so bad, why was he so late discovering it? Was he that out of touch? There are better ways to handle situations like that. (It just so happens that that dad had just experienced had a huge spiritual renewal and turnaround in his life; but because of lack of spiritual maturity and over-zealousness, he made a tragic mistake with his daughter.)

Dad, if your teenage daughter ever asks you to listen to her new CD that she thinks is just great, you've got a big opportunity staring you in the face. Don't blow it. You know you're probably not going to like it and probably won't even understand a word of it. She tells you to sit down in the floor, close your eyes and listen. Do it and don't act like you dread it. When it's over, say something like "I can see why you like that. That was some driving beat! Who are they anyway? How'd you hear about 'em? They're gonna be huge! What were they saying anyway?" She'll say something like, "Oh, I don't know, but aren't they just great?" Then she'll tell you they're coming to town and tickets are only $95 each and she'd like you to take her and some friends to hear them. Start saving your money, pop!

I've said some of this in earlier sessions, but it's worth repeating. *Make* friends with your kids and *stay* friends with them. Talk to them a lot, but don't glare at them in the eyes—they find that threatening and intrusive; avoid constant questioning—use statements, comments, observations instead; show an interest in their school activities, homework assignments, reports, teachers, coaches; be available to your kids—don't make them think they're a bother or they'll avoid you; seek out their opinions, thoughts, advice; don't insult or embarrass them; be predictable and consistent; encourage healthy relationships; try to have some fun in your family; expect the best of your kids and let them know it; keep them close to you without smothering them; don't express fear that they're going to go wild in their teenage years. Whew! Your kids have got to know that you will always be in their corner pulling for them and that out of 6.79 billion

people on the planet, you're the best friend they'll ever have!

Here are some scriptures I want to use in closing this lesson. James 1:26 says, *"Anyone who says he's a Christian but doesn't control his sharp tongue is just fooling himself, and his religion isn't worth much."* And Proverbs 15:1 says, *"A soft answer turns away wrath."* The underlying teaching here is "attitude." Attitudes are a reflection of our thinking and reveal themselves in what we say, how we say it and how we act.

> *You must be in authority over your kids—just don't be an authoritarian who's got to pull every string in their journey to independence.*

Now let's get back to that "perfect storm" again. If you're a true storm-chaser and want to experience a perfect storm at home firsthand, just do the following sixteen things with your kids. "But this isn't fun!" No, but maybe it'll get the point across.

1. Avoid your kids; don't talk to them much or show much interest in what they're doing.
2. Embarrass them, especially in front of their peers.
3. Be extremely rigid and critical.
4. Be close-minded in your positions and opinions and not sympathetic to theirs.
5. Bully them, pull rank on them, constantly remind them who's boss.
6. Become known for a NO face and a NO attitude.
7. Speak with a harsh, curt tone of voice.
8. Be disrespectful of their feelings, opinions and desires.
9. Let them see you speak to and treat your spouse disrespectfully.
10. Let them witness serious conflict between you and your spouse.
11. Make your kids ask for everything they need instead of stepping up to meet some of their needs before they even have a chance to ask.
12. Be cheap and stingy; leave the generous attitude to someone else.
13. Don't apologize and say "I'm sorry" even when you and everybody else knows you're wrong.
14. Question your kids relentlessly.
15. Talk one way—walk another way.

16. Backslide spiritually—take the feet out from under your faith.

Now I know you're not expecting to have a *perfect home* any more than I am. We're all imperfect people whom God loves with the greatest of all hearts. He wants the best for us. And I know you don't want a *perfect storm* to come barreling through your home. So consider this: **A Christ-like attitude planted firmly in your mind and heart is your best protection against** *that storm.* In Romans 12:2 (NLT), the Apostle Paul says, *"Don't copy the behavior and customs of the world, but let God transform you into a new person by changing the way you think. Then you will know what God wants you to do, and you will know how good and pleasing and perfect his will really is."*

What a difference attitude makes! Especially at home—where everybody's growing up together.

DISCUSSION

1. Share some of your own thoughts about the importance of "attitude" in the home. What are some examples of positive and negative attitudes you're picking up in the home? Any of them coming from teenagers? What are you hearing?

_____
_____
_____

2. Talk for a moment about what's behind or what's motivating negatives attitudes. Are you sensing dissatisfaction, confusion, irritation, undue pressure and stress, unrealistic expectations? Where is this coming from? What positive attitudes are you picking up on?

_____
_____
_____

3. Discuss for a moment what you feel teenagers really want *most* where they are in life. List five things you'd definitely put at the top of their list, then share your thoughts.

   a. _____
   b. _____
   c. _____
   d. _____
   e. _____

4. Now zero in on five of the biggest issues or problems you think teenagers are dealing with today. Discuss as a group. Adjust your list as necessary.

   a. _____
   b. _____
   c. _____
   d. _____
   e. _____

5. Speak from experience now. What do you think it takes to create an atmosphere at home that makes teenagers feel comfortable? Who has the burden of responsibility? If things aren't going well, what might you do to make things better?

_____

_____

_____

6. What role do Bible teaching, mentoring, church activities, and Christian friends play in your teenagers' lives? What's it going to take to keep them active in church? What can you do?

_____

_____

_____

5-DAY ACTION PLAN

DAY 1: *Your action today is to be aware of your attitudes at home, work, wherever you are.* Ask yourself if you are by nature a positive "look for the best, think the best" type person or are you more of "this won't work, no use trying, I see problems galore" type person. Do you automatically think the best and tend to respond, or do you tend to think the worst and tend to react negatively? We know that things that appear negative don't necessarily express negative attitudes. In fact, "no" can be just as positive as "yes" in many situations. But the question is: What is your basic outlook on life? Is it positive or negative? What jumps out at you first—problems or potential? Today, **be aware of your attitudes** as you go about your regular activities. Our attitudes are reflected in our words and actions.

DAY 2: Today, *consider how your children's attitudes are developing*. We're not talking about psychoanalysis here. Just ask yourself: Are your kids generally pretty optimistic, easily encouraged, motivated, able to get excited about things? Are they cautious, suspicious, reluctant to get excited, afraid they might be disappointed? All kids come into the world wired differently, and that's a blessing. We parents just have to be discerning and look for their strengths in order to encourage them. Tune in to your kids and *consider how their attitudes are developing*.

DAY 3: If you're going through challenging times with your teenagers, hopefully, something in this lesson has resonated with you. None of us has been, is or will be a perfect parent. Nor will our kids be perfect. But today,

zero in on two or three things that might improve your situation at home. Maybe some external factors are in play, relationships with friends, or something going on at school. Be honest with yourself and focus in on the truth as best you can identify it. If part of the problem lies with you, try to correct it. If the atmosphere at home is tense, try to implement some of our ideas and look for improvement. *Zero in on two or three things that might improve your situation at home*.

DAY 4: Teenagers want to feel valued, considered and listened to. They're moving toward independence, yet don't really have the experience or assets to be there yet. Today, *focus on treating your teenagers with utmost respect and attention*. How can you make their

> Today, focus on treating your teenagers with utmost respect and attention.

day a little less complicated? Kids need help, advice, direction, etc., but don't always want to ask for it. Step into that teenager's life casually and see if you can help with anything. Then when *you* really need some help, ask *him* to help *you*. And be sure to thank him. Just interact wherever, whenever and however you can in a casual, non-threatening way. Teenagers today are smart and often feel like they're taken for granted just because they're teenagers. *Treat your teenagers with utmost respect and attention today*. You may need some help with your computer!

DAY 5: *Focus today on Romans 12:2 and how it pertains to your thinking and attitudes.* Consider the influence our secular culture is exerting on us—all of us, not just our kids—and how God has changed each of us into a new person by changing the way we think. The secular world is trying to conform us to its value system, but God's plan for believers is to transform them to embrace His value system. As you think on this scripture truth today and in the days ahead, you'll know more clearly what God wants you to think and do, and how satisfying it is to live within His will. *Today, focus on Romans 12:2 and how it pertains to your thinking and attitudes.*

PRAYER

Father, thank You for my family. We haven't solved every problem that's come along, but we're not through yet. And You're not through working in us. I am confident I can grow in patience and understanding as I try to be the parent my children need and deserve. In Jesus' name—Amen.

LESSON
6

WHAT A DIFFERENCE BIRTH ORDER MAKES!
Understanding Our Uniqueness and Making the Most of It

SCRIPTURE:

Psalm 139:13-14

Jeremiah 1:5

Matthew 10:30

REFLECTION

Our topic today is one I've talked about for years now. In fact, *The Birth Order Book* I wrote in the mid-80's has sold well over a million copies. Remember a guy named Phil Donahue? He was around long before Oprah. Back in 1985, I did a segment on birth order on his show, and the response was so good, it was later replayed on the "Best of Donahue." People are interested in birth order.

So—we're talking about birth order in this lesson, and how important it is to understand our uniqueness and make the most of it. And this is not just about kids— it's about adults as well.

As we've already said, all children come into this world wired differently. We've seen that in some Bible characters from the same families: Cain and Abel; Jacob and Esau; Joseph and his brothers; Martha and Mary. They were all uniquely different. Some siblings today are rough and tough, while others will melt before your eyes; some are studious, others are athletic; some are

super smart, while others drop out of school and get rich. We're all different from the start. That's God's plan.

In addition to being a dean of students at The University of Arizona, I taught graduate level courses in counseling and psychology. Students would come to my classes in droves because I taught using real families, real married couples with real kids. We'd talk about issues they were dealing with, why they did what they did and how to make changes for the better. People found it fascinating that their little cubbies could come out of the same den and yet be so different.

Our key scripture, Psalm 139:13-14 says, "You made all the delicate, inner parts of my body and knit me together in my mother's womb. Thank you for making me so wonderfully complex! Your workmanship is marvelous—and how well I know it."

A baby's view of life begins to take shape the moment he arrives on the scene. How does this happen? Well, think about it. When the firstborn comes home – who are his role models? Parents—adults. And that new baby is the parents' "guinea pig." They're going to learn the ropes of parenting with this first child, responding to every cry immediately, planning every detail of the baby's day. As the little first-born guy gets older, he develops a need to know exactly what his day holds in store. He doesn't like surprises. When he wonders, "What time are we leaving?"...you don't answer "Somewhere around 9:30." He wants you to be a little more specific than that.

...all children come into this world wired differently.

Think back to the way you documented the births of your children. For that first one, you've got a baby book filled out from front to back; the second one's baby book is halfway filled out; and the third one's baby book is still in the original box unopened. What's interesting is that the firstborn child models the conscientious traits of the parents. He or she is orderly, a list maker, and comes to expect that needs are going to be met with certainty and swiftness.

Firstborn children are groomed for success. They seem to be natural leaders who learn to dominate their surroundings because they go unchallenged within the first few years of life. Consider this: Of the first twenty-three astronauts in our space program, twenty-one were firstborn children. The other two were only-children. The fact is, your first child has just about everything going for him—that is, until he hears some news around the house—"Guess what, Joe Bob! You're going to have a baby sister."

When we look into the newborn face of that *second child*, we automatically think, "Hey, this baby doesn't look at all like the first one!" Well, should she? People just seem to expect a replica of the first child. When teachers are checking roll on the first day of school and see the last name of a kid they had before, they may be elated—or terrified—to think that the same mold has surfaced a second time. But of course, most teachers know better.

When the second child comes home, the firstborn wonders why this little bundle of trouble has invaded his territory, and sibling rivalry begins ramping up as

two kids are now in competition for their parent's attention. The wise parent will go to that older child and point out things such as, "Look at that baby—can she walk?" "No," he'll say. "But you *can* walk. And how many naps do you take a day?" "One," the older child will say. "Think about how many naps the new baby has to take—eight!" "See, you're the big brother now, and you're going to get to help your little sister grow up. Maybe you can teach her how to do some of the things you can do—like choke the dog and flush the goldfish!" Seriously, you want to affirm your older child and his position with relation to the younger child.

As soon as the second child starts to crawl, she lands in the middle of big brother's stuff. She's the rough and tumble competitor who realizes that when she wants certain toys to play with, snatching them away from big brother seems like the best option. And she will use those toys in a way that never occurred to the older brother. In a word, middle children tend to march to the beat of a different drummer, and they are more likely to be strong-willed and rebellious. Statistics show that they have a tendency toward becoming entrepreneurs. Some of today's most successful business innovators are middle children. From biblical characters such as Cain and Abel to some recent U.S. presidents and their brothers, history shows that the firstborn and second child will see life through different lenses. And to further complicate matters, the parents once again announce, "Guess what? We're going to have a baby!" Suddenly, the second child is going to be the *middle child*.

Well, this baby of the family—Little Schnooky, as I like to call him—goes through life looking *up*! He must figure out how to get attention over and above the shenanigans of his older siblings. But this last-born youngster is likely to be the most social of the bunch, never meeting a stranger. He becomes adept at being manipulative and jumping into situations with both feet and asking questions later. Research shows that youngest children are top salesmen, and many times turn out to be the comedians of the family. Some of America's most popular comedians are babies of their families who capitalized on their ability to entertain and make people laugh.

Have you ever had the feeling that you should treat all of your children the same? Whether you live in Montana, Texas, or Virginia, the state you live in will treat your 16-year-old a little different from the way it treats your 14-year-old. Life treats people differently, according to where they are in the progression of life. As parents, we don't need to be afraid to treat our children differently concerning curfews, bed times, allowances, chores, TV and computer time, cell phone privileges, driving the car, etc. Core beliefs, values, and principles of right and wrong remain consistent, but privileges should vary according to age and maturity. Whenever possible, some of the chores of the older children should be passed down to the younger children as older kids' lives become more complicated and they are granted more independence for making their own decisions.

Ask yourself this question: Does God give us all the same gifts to work with in life? Does He expect the exact same thing of all of us? No, He designed each of us to be unique, with our own personalities, abilities, interests, appearance and potential. In Jeremiah 1:5, the Lord says, *"I knew you before I formed you in your mother's womb. Before you were born, I set you apart...."* Matt. 10:30 says, *"And the very hairs on your head are all numbered."*

Knowing that each child is distinctive gives parents an opportunity to point out that God has a plan that is specific to each child. Does God expect us to meet the same standard when we come to faith in Christ, to learn and practice godly values, to live obediently to his Word? Yes. But one of the great privileges of parenting is that of recognizing our children's distinct differences and turn them into advantages—showing no favoritism to which one happens to be the smartest, the most athletic or the most attractive.

Let me give you three variables that affect birth order.

- **Sex of the children** – If you have two girls and then have a son, he will generally display the traits of the firstborn child.

- **Physical characteristics** – When the younger children are physically bigger and taller than the older child, the older child may submit to their leadership rather than try to lead them.

- **Critical eye** – Here is a variable that can do a lot of damage. Parents with an overly critical eye—I call them *flawpickers*—tend to find some little something wrong with everything a child does. Parents who pick at the flaws or mistakes of the firstborn child may very well wind up with a kid who is unreliable, unconscientious, or maybe even a "slob" who never

gets anything done, much less done right. Why? Because he's so afraid he'll be criticized. He's already accustomed to being picked to pieces! In his mind, he'll say "I'll just make a practice of not finishing things. That way I can't possibly be criticized." Parents, here's the lesson, and you need to learn it: If you're a flawpicker, there's a good chance you'll raise a kid who's going to go through life putting himself down. Trust me—don't be a flawpicker!

Are we trying to raise perfect kids? Certainly not. The goal is to raise a child who's a pursuer of *excellence* rather than a pursuer of *perfection*. A perfectionist sets up standards in which he is bound to fail. It has been said that "perfectionism is a slow way to die." You're bound to fail somewhere along the way. You can't achieve perfection! And even if you could, no one would recognize it because no one has seen it! The pursuer of excellence, on the other hand, has high standards and tries hard to reach them. There's a big difference here. One way to determine which of these you are as a parent is to ask yourself how you respond to criticism. The pursuer of excellence welcomes criticism, is not threatened, is open to suggestions, and feels better-equipped to achieve his goals. When the perfectionist is criticized or fails, he often simply shuts down, feeling frustrated and disappointed in himself.

A baby's view of life begins to take shape the moment he arrives on the scene.

Here are some more things you need to know about birth order that will help you raise rock-solid kids.

1. *Firstborn*—Remember, firstborns need to know specifics. Don't give them too much responsibility for their age, or they will "skip" childhood altogether. Be careful about over-correcting or micromanaging them. If you turn them into perfectionists, you'll end up with kids who will feel defeated at every turn. Also, be careful not to "should" your firstborn. Don't say "you *should* do this, you *should* do that over and over." In other words, what they're doing is never enough. Instead, project just the opposite—"I love you just the way you are."

2. *Middle child*—Middle children need to be listened to! Ask their opinion about anything, e.g., vacation

planning, décor, purchases, etc. Enjoy two-on-one time, where both mom and dad spend time with the middle child. Look for exclusive territory, even if it's "Honey, why don't you pick the restaurant?" Let the middle child know, "Hey, we respect you as an individual, and we value your opinions." If you do, you'll neutralize some of the competitive spirit that is naturally there.

3. *Lastborn*—Lastborns need to be given the opportunity to lead, perhaps in family outings or in planning celebrations. The babies of the family will have much to compare themselves to, so affirmation is crucial. If lastborns feel less academic or less athletic than the older siblings, help them identify and develop their own unique strengths. Enjoy lastborns' social skills, laugh *with* them and *at* them as they entertain you, and remind them that every gift of life is God-given.

Only-children are in a class by themselves. By the time they're in the second grade, age 7 or 8, they function as pint-sized adults. The secret here is not to let these kids get too far ahead of themselves.

Another intriguing combination of children is *identical twins*. Why God created two kids out of the same DNA but gave them different fingerprints, I'll never know! I guess it's His way of saying, "You may look just like your sister, but there's really no one else like you." People spend billions of dollars every year trying to be like and look like other people; but no matter how much money they spend, they are uniquely *themselves*. It's when they artificially try to *be* someone else that trouble begins.

Well, there you are: A few thoughts on birth order. Just remember, we're all *who* God made us to be, and we should praise Him for making each of us so wonderfully different and complex. Whether your kids are the firstborn, middle child, lastborn, only child, twins or something in between, let each one know that he or she is truly special to you and that you'll always be their #1 fan! Birth order does make a difference. Let's thank God for our uniqueness and make the most of it!

DISCUSSION

1. Reflecting on Psalm 139:13-14, do you think most children and adults see their differences as "marvelous"? How can you use the truth of this verse to help children appreciate their differences and use them to their advantage? Share your thoughts.

_____

_____

_____

2. As parents, we sometimes struggle with the fact that our children's personalities, tastes and characteristics are so varied. What about the home you were raised in? Were the differences between siblings ever challenging to you or your parents? How did you deal with it?

_____

_____

_____

3. If you are married, how would you describe your and your spouse's differences in terms of what each of you brings to the marriage? Are you able to blend your differences harmoniously? How do you find balance?

_____

_____

_____

4. In your experience, when do you think sibling rivalry begins? What can you do to keep the firstborn from feeling set aside when the second child comes along? Any who have experience with this should speak up. Make some notes.

_____

_____

_____

5. Understanding some of the characteristics of birth order helps us recognize our children's uniqueness and make the most of it. Beside each descriptive word below, write a 1, 2, 3 or 4 to indicate whether that word is applicable to the firstborn, middle child, last-born or only child.

____ Manipulative	____ Leader	____ Comedian
____ Great Communicator	____ Entrepreneur	____ Adult-like
____ Rough & Tumble	____ Dominates	____ Follows rules

6. Regardless of birth order and different abilities and personality traits, we need to recognize that God loves each of us the same. As a group, share a few of the unique qualities you recognize in your children and how these qualities can contribute to a successful, productive life in the future. Jot down some thoughts.

_____

_____

_____

5-DAY ACTION PLAN

DAY 1: *Today, focus on yourself and thank God that you are "you" and that He designed you to be no one but "you."* Consider your own personal traits and characteristics, and also the kind of family you grew up in and how you related to your siblings. Are you able to associate any birth order characteristics with members of the family you grew up in? Where did you seem to fit in the scheme of things? *Today, focus on yourself and thank God that you are "you" and that He designed you to be no one but "you."*

DAY 2: If you are a parent, *try to identify birth order characteristics in each of your children.* Are they firstborn, middle child, lastborn, only child, twins? Consider their personality traits, how they relate to one another and to you as a parent. Make some notes on each child and update them with observations regularly. Mark their progress and development. The goal is to know your children's strengths and abilities so you can "train them up in the way they should go." Today, *try to identify the birth order characteristics in each of your children.*

DAY 3: If you are married, *consider how your birth*

order and/or personal characteristics affect your <u>marriage</u>. Are you leaders? Are you pushers? Are you result-oriented, organized, driven, laid back, patient, impatient, opinionated? Are you a collaborator, a management type, perfectionist, procrastinator, aggressive, quiet, efficient, creative, etc.? How do you see yourselves? More importantly, how do you work together as a married couple to complement each other's personali-

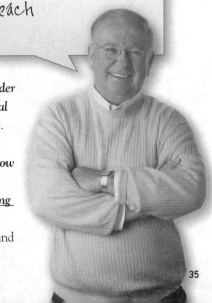

Try to identify the birth order characteristics in each of your children.

ties in a respectful way? Today, *consider how your birth order and/or personal characteristics affect your marriage.*

DAY 4: If you are married, *consider how birth order and/or personal characteristics directly affect your* <u>parenting style</u>. The type person you are, what you believe, how you think, reason and act will greatly affect how you rear your children. As we have already said, all children are different. And that's a good thing. Try to harmonize your personal traits with theirs so you can be consistent, patient encouragers instead of inconsistent, impatient drivers. Work in harmony with each other and your children as your family grows up together. Today, *consider how your and your spouse's birth order and/or personal characteristics affect your parenting style*.

DAY 5: Very important: *Focus today on your personal spiritual life*. Whatever age you happen to be, there's one thing you can be sure of: Your relationship with Jesus Christ will affect every area of your life. It is the single most crucial success factor in a satisfying life, a healthy marriage and happy family. If you're married, the kind of Christian life you lead will directly affect the lives of your children. As a parent, ask yourself: If my children grow up to be just like me, will that be a great thing? A good thing? An OK thing? Or do I need to make some course corrections? Whether you're single or married, your greatest desire in life should be to live for Christ. If you have children, your desire should be to have a happy family and raise *respectful, responsible* and *resourceful* kids who follow Christ. Very important: *Focus today on your personal spiritual life*. If it's not where you want it to be, I hope you will get busy and do something about it. Your family will be blessed.

PRAYER

Father, thank You for the life You have given me and every member of my family. Help me to recognize and appreciate my own uniqueness and that of my children so that together we can pursue the paths you have planned for us. In Jesus' name—Amen.

LESSON

7

WHAT A DIFFERENCE GRANDPARENTS MAKE!

Working Together to Make Grandparenting "Grand"

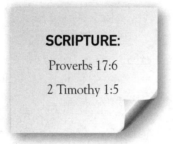

SCRIPTURE:

Proverbs 17:6

2 Timothy 1:5

REFLECTION

You already know that I think being a grandparent is great. When you think about it, one of the things that makes it so special is that it takes a long time to become one. You can become a mother or father in a few months, but becoming a grandparent takes years! I've asked myself, "Leman, what's really so special about having grandkids?" Well, the fact they belong to someone else isn't exactly #1, but it's not far behind! Seriously, it's just very satisfying to see a new generation come alive right before your eyes. It's like watching your own kids grow up in someone else's home. Sandy and I have two grandchildren: Conner is nine, and Adeline is seven. Talk about night and day different. Wow! And watching our children raise them is almost like seeing ourselves in action.

Proverbs 17:6 (NLT) says, *"Grandchildren are the crowning glory of the aged; parents are the pride of their children."* Now I'm not too fond of that word "aged." Sounds ancient. How about the "...crowning glory of their 'grandparents'"? Better. After years in the trenches raising our kids, we get a crown of glory in the form of grandchildren. Sweet thought.

One day I was walking our youngest daughter, Lauren, to school, and a guy says to me, "Ah, I've got a grandchild in this school, too." I usually let this kind of thing pass since we had our little shock bundle at age 48. (And by the way, at 48 there's no labor at all. One sneeze and you're there!) Well, anyway, the man said, "I've got a grandchild in this school, too." I replied, "Actually, sir, this is number five for me." He said, "Oh, five grandchildren! Aren't you lucky?" I was blessed indeed.

Now here's my message to you as a grandparent: Be determined to make a difference in your grandkids' lives through your role as a grandmother or grandfather. Your influence should be lasting and rewarding. And grandkids can't make this happen. Only you and the children's parents can, by working together.

We live in a culture these days that's really quite disturbing. Way too many parents have bailed out on their kids and left them high and dry even though they're all still under the same roof. There's partying, alcohol, drugs, dissension, spousal abuse, fighting, wife-swapping, custody battles, you name it. God alone knows. And the kids are helpless. I tell you, if you let yourself think much about it, it'll make you cry. Thank God—thank God!—there are lots of parents and grandparents out there who are doing things right! Are their kids fortunate or what?! And to have godly grandparents who are willing to step up to the plate and into their grandkids' lives—WOW! What a blessing. The attitude beating in their heart and mind is "We *can* make a difference, and we *will*!"

You can become a mother or father in a few months, but becoming a grandparent takes years!

What kind of things do you do with your grandkids? One thing you can do is tell them stories. It's amazing how they'll listen and never forget the characters and story line. Do things repetitively with them. One of the ways kids learn best is through repetition. Games, songs, stories, pictures, whatever—they work. Watch some of their favorite movies with them and comment on something different each time. Sometimes you'll find teachable moments there.

Keep grandkids close by being affectionate with them. They love your hugs and enjoy hearing how much you love them. Just don't fall into the trap of thinking you have to buy their affection. They'll remember you a lot longer for what you *do with* them rather than for what all you *give* them. They need your attention, encouragement and approval. After all, their parents are YOUR children! They may not say it, but they expect wisdom, sound thinking and good advice from you. *You* are a person of experience to them. After all, you've lived the *longest*, so you should know the *most*. Support them in their dreams and ideas. Look for teachable moments when you're with them—just don't get preachy. It turns them off.

Now this is for step-grandparents. Families are changing all right, and this means more step-children, step-parents and step-grandparents. Blending families can

be challenging, taking an average of three to seven years to blend comfortably. But it seems they can collide overnight! And inevitably, kids are caught in the blender and can get pureed in the process. Just accept the fact that while you may or may not hit it off with everybody in the stepfamily, you've still got to respect them. And don't expect your step-grandchildren to automatically love you or call you grandpa or grandma. That may not happen. What you must do, however, is to try to have a relationship with them that is built on mutual respect.

Naturally, if you live near your grandkids, you'll see them more. If you're not close, you've got email, Facebook, FaceTime, Skype, texting and all that. Plus, you can write them "actual" letters, send greeting cards, stickers for little kids, and even slip in a $20 bill every now and then. That'll keep them opening the mail. Always include something like "I'm praying for you; I'm thinking about you; I want to hear about school, soccer, dance recital, whatever." They love knowing that you care about them. Remember, you're bigger than life! Too many grandparents never really understand the impact they can have on grandkids. I'm telling you, it can be huge.

If you don't live close to your grandkids, arrange for them to come to see you, maybe stay a couple of months. Maybe you're bored and want them to pack in for five or six months. Their parents will perk up to that! Take them on a camping trip, fishing, nighttime walks, to the zoo, the circus, children's museums, you name it. Have them over for a special craft day or to help you build something in your workshop. Teach them how to milk a cow. Of course, you'll have to learn how—after you find a cow!

Several years ago I wrote "A Child's Ten Commandments" that was picked up in a Dear Abby column. I'm told that 55 million people read it. Now it's time to follow up with "A Grandparent's Ten Commandments." We might even call it "How to Make Grandparenting 'Grand'."

1. **Treat each of your grandchildren according to their unique characteristics, interests and abilities**. They're all different. Naturally, core values such as love, care, boundaries, principles of behavior, etc., remain the same for all of them, but recognizing their differences makes them feel special.

2. **Communicate with them and show interest in**

everything about them – their school, their friendships, their activities, their ideas, thoughts and faith.

3. **Live an exemplary life.** The grandkids are watching you and listening to you. Your thoughts and opinions carry weight with them.

4. **Always be gracious and complimentary of the other set of grandparents.** And don't get in a competitive "giving" contest with the other grandparents.

5. **Offer to have the grandkids overnight or take them on a short trip.**

6. **Come up with some creative ideas and special things to do with them, maybe that no one else has ever done with them.** That will keep them thinking you're cool. Don't assume that parents have already taught the kids how to do everything, because they haven't. Probably haven't had time. Remember, if you don't act like a geezer, the grandkids won't see you as a geezer!

7. **Send letters or notes with pictures, illustrations you've drawn, or stickers for the little ones.** And for older kids, unmarked bills will do just fine.

8. **Always expect the best and let your grandkids know you have high hopes and expectations of them.** Project "I'm just certain you're going to be outstanding in whatever you do!"

9. **Pray for them every day and always look for ways to lay the groundwork for their coming to Christ, if they haven't already.** Talk about how important it is to live for Christ. The Apostle Paul said to Timothy in 2 Timothy 1:5, *"I am reminded of your sincere faith, a faith that dwelt first in your grandmother Lois and your mother Eunice and now, I am sure, dwells in you as well."* Grandmother and granddad, hand your faith down—keep it alive and moving through the generations that follow you.

10. Then, finally, **consider creating a DVD or video of some of your thoughts and experiences for your adult kids and grandchildren to remember you by.** This will be a keepsake. You can probably even do it using the camera on your cell phone.

They'll remember you a lot longer for what you do with them rather than for what all you give them.

Now let me make some suggestions to *parents* on how to make grandparenting "grand."

1. **Always speak positively about the grandparents, never critical or demeaning.**

2. **Treat grandparents with love and respect, especially in front of the children.** The kids will learn to love their grandparents the way you as parents love them.

3. **Call on the grandparents for help and assistance when you need them, but always express appreciation, if possible, in front of the children.**

4. **Don't take advantage of grandparents.** They have lives and responsibilities of their own. Always give them a way out when you call on them for help. They may be dealing with some big changes in life, and in some cases, may not have a lot of life left. At some point, they will likely become dependent in the same way children are dependent. Don't wear them out.

5. **Let your children see the way you love and show concern for your parents (the grandparents) as a model so they'll know how to treat you in your later years.**

6. **Always stay tuned in to the needs of the grandparents.** You have a big obligation to them. Unless you were adopted, *they are the reason you are alive.* They deserve your love and respect.

Can you really have a new family by Friday? Sure you can, even if today is Thursday! Can you really make grandparenting "grand"? Absolutely you can, and working together makes all the difference. In the mean time, you can give 'em love, give 'em sugar and give 'em back! How sweet it is to be a grandparent! I wouldn't trade it for the world!

DISCUSSION

1. Discuss for a few moments any unique roles grandparents played in the lives of your group. Were any in the group raised by grandparents? From both the parents' and grandparents' point of view, what's so special about grandkids and why?

   _____

   _____

   _____

2. If you have children, how would you describe the relationship your children have with their grandparents? If it's good, what steps have you taken to make it so?

   _____

   _____

   _____

3. Jot down what you consider to be three significant contributions grandparents can make to the children in your family.

   a. _____

   b. _____

   c. _____

4. How do you feel the relationship between parents and grandparents in your family is going? What have you tried to do to build a strong relationship, not just between you and them, but between the kids and them? How do you handle distance issues?

   _____

   _____

   _____

5. Do you feel good about the way you interact with your parents so your kids have a positive model as to how aging parents/grandparents should be treated? How *should* they be treated?

   _____

   _____

   _____

6. Grandparents, how do you handle discipline issues involving grandkids' behavior or speech that you feel needs to be corrected? Do you have a clear understanding or boundaries regarding discipline, or is there just an "unspoken understanding" of how discipline should be handled? Talk about this as a group and share ideas.

   _____

   _____

7. Do you see 2 Timothy 1:5 being played out in your family? If so, how? If not, how would you like to see it played out?

   _____

   _____

5-DAY ACTION PLAN

DAY 1: Today, *focus on your personal experience with your own grandparents.* Think about what you learned from them or see/saw in them that made a lasting impression on you. Was it positive and helpful? Consider things they did or said that may have helped shape who you are today. If they're still active in your life, contact them and tell them how much you appreciate them. Today, *focus on your personal experience with your own grandparents.* Pause and say a prayer of thanks for them. After all, if it weren't for them….

DAY 2: Grandparents, nothing is better than being able to love on the grandkids, share special activities with them and make good memories together. Today, *do something special with or for your grandkids*—not with a gift or anything tangible necessarily. Just contact them by phone, email, text, a personal visit, whatever, to reassure them of how much they mean to you. Whether you have one or a dozen grandkids, today, let them know that they occupy a special place in your life. *Do something special with or for your grandkids today.*

DAY 3: Your action today is to *make a list of some interesting activities you can do that involve the grandkids.* And be <u>creative</u>. Naturally, their ages will determine what you plan. Push the envelope a bit and venture into areas they might really find interesting and enlightening, and that might reveal some interest or ability they have and might even want to pursue later. We're talking about more than ordinary stuff like going to a movie or watching a video with them. You can do that anytime. *Make a list of some interesting activities you can do that involve the grandkids.* You might be surprised at what you can come up with. Be creative and think young.

DAY 4: Parents, your action today is to *have your children do something special and specific for the grandparents*—something that shows their love and appreciation. Maybe it's mailing them a letter or a card they've made, sending a text, inviting them over for a meal, etc. Just make it real and natural and let it come from the hearts of the kids themselves. Today, *have your children do something special for the grandparents*—maybe one set of grandparents today and one set tomorrow. Appreciation is never a waste.

DAY 5: *Grandparents, find a way to reach out to the other grandparents* who might not be involved in this study. Personally, I look for ways to affirm the other grandparents for their contribution to our children's lives as well as the grandkids' lives. Again, any type of communication will work—a call, text, email. Just let them know that you share a common interest in the well-being of the family and that having a happy, Christ-centered home is all you've ever wanted for your children and grandchildren. Today, *find a way to reach out to the other grandparents.*

SUMMARY

Well, we've covered a lot of ground in this study on the family. I've tried the best I know how to help you and encourage you—whether you're married, single, parents or grandparents. You see, I believe the most effective witness the world will ever see is the combined witness of a Christian family. To me, nothing else comes close. I think the reason is that within the home and family God's principles can be tested and proven to work so beautifully. And others can see it. Two things I ask you to do. The first is: Follow through with the 5-Day Action Plans. The goal is for you to carry them beyond the individual days and into your life permanently. The second is: Pray for each person in your family, and treat them with love and respect and a kind heart. In Ephesians 4:32 (NLT), the Apostle Paul says, "Be kind to each other, tenderhearted, forgiving one another, even as God through Christ has forgiven you." What a great way to live and have a happier family! Best wishes always.

— Kevin Leman

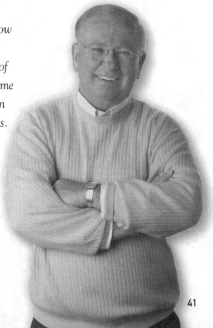

PRAYER

Father, thank you for the insights I've gained from this study. I believe with all my heart that it doesn't *have* to take months or years to see a happier family. We can have it starting today. I promise to love and respect and care for every member of my family, and I will do all I can to help them reach their true potential in life. Thank you for the life and hope You have given me and my family—through Jesus Christ our Lord. In His name I pray—Amen.

NOTES

NOTES

NOTES

NOTES

NOTES